That's the FACT Jack!

A COLLECTION OF 101
STRANGE BUT TRUE
FACTS!

MICHAEL SCHLUETER

That's the **FACT** Jack!

MICHAEL SCHLUETER
Copyright 2018 Michael Schlueter

ISBN 978-1-71800-289-0

DEDICATION

For my beautiful children, Amanda and Chase.
I hope the wonder and beauty of life fascinates
and inspires you every day.

That's the **F̲A̲C̲T̲** Jack!

Strange? Yes!
Weird?   Sometimes!
Crazy?   Usually!

but ....

Truth *I̲S̲* stranger than fiction!!

You can't make this stuff up!!

Sometimes there are facts that just make us
shake our heads in wonder and disbelief. That
seem too outrageous to be true - but yet they
are!
If you get a kick out of these oddities as much
as I do, you're sure to enjoy this collection!
Share a few with your family and friends to
impress them with your incredible knowledge or
just to see the expression on their face!

Hope you enjoy!

Michael

STRANGE BUT TRUE

"The Empire State Building in New York gets struck by lightning about 23 times a year."

This building (the third tallest in New York City) actually acts as a lightning rod for the surrounding area.

STRANGE BUT TRUE

"The color green used to be considered unlucky in Ireland since it was associated with fairies who stole children and brides."

In time, however, the color green became popular in Ireland due to Ireland's nickname as "The Emerald Isle," the green in the Irish flag, and the clover that St. Patrick used in his teachings about Catholicism.

3

STRANGE BUT TRUE

"The oldest recipe in existence is a recipe for beer."

In Mesopotamia (ancient Iraq), a 3900-year-old Sumerian poem honoring Ninkasi, the patron goddess of brewing, contains the oldest surviving beer recipe, describing the production of beer from barley via bread.

STRANGE BUT TRUE

"In the average lifetime, a person will walk the equivalent of five times around the equator."

That distance would equal approximately 124,510 miles!

STRANGE BUT TRUE

"You can compete in an underwater mountain bike race in Wales, United Kingdom!"

Riders compete in the 'World Mountain Bike Bog Snorkeling Championship' where competitors have to ride a mountain bike as fast as they can along the bottom of Waen Rhydd Bog, a six and a half feet deep water-filled trench. The bikes are specially prepared with lead-filled frames and riders wear lead weight belts to avoid floating off the bikes.

The event has been run for 32 years!

STRANGE BUT TRUE

"The first archaeological evidence of soup comes from 6000B.C. and its primary ingredient was hippopotamus."

Not sure exactly how it wound up being the ingredient of choice!
Bon Appetit!

STRANGE BUT TRUE

"A lightning bolt generates temperatures five times hotter than those found at the sun's surface!"

A lightning bolt's temperature can reach approximately 53,540 degrees Fahrenheit, while the surface temperature of the sun is just 10,340 degrees Fahrenheit.

STRANGE BUT TRUE

"One side of the Nobel Peace Prize medal depicts three naked men with their hands on each other's shoulders!"

This depiction is meant to represent the 'fraternal bond of men.'

The other side of the coin depicts a bust of Alfred Nobel, the Swedish chemist, engineer, and industrialist who invented dynamite and founded the Nobel prizes.

STRANGE BUT TRUE

"A 'jiffy' is an actual unit of time equal to the time it takes light to travel one centimeter in a vacuum (approximately 33.3564 picoseconds)!"
Or approximately 1/100th of a second!

When someone tells you, they'll be with you in a 'jiffy', now you'll know how long that will really be!

STRANGE BUT TRUE

"Bacteria can grow and divide every 20 minutes, turning one bacterial cell into 16 million in just eight hours!"

The bacteria we know most about is E. coli. If conditions were optimum (warm, lots of nutrients) it could divide and multiply exponentially. After one day there would be more bacteria than there are grains of sand on all of the world's beaches! Thankfully for us, these optimal conditions never exist for any length of time!

STRANGE BUT TRUE

"If you counted 24 hours a day, it would take 31,688 years to reach one trillion!"

Better start counting now if you want this one crossed off your bucket list!

STRANGE BUT TRUE

"A 100-pound woman wearing stiletto heels exerts more pressure on the ground than a 6000-pound elephant!"

The pressure of her step is eight times as much, or 240 pounds per square inch instead of 30 pounds per square inch!

Physics – gotta love it!

STRANGE BUT TRUE

"Until 1796, there was a state in the United States called Franklin. Today it's known as Tennessee!"

Franklin was created in 1784 from territory offered by North Carolina as a cession to Congress to help pay off debts related to the American War of Independence. It was founded with the intent of becoming the fourteenth state of the new United States.

STRANGE BUT TRUE

"In the year 2000, Pope John Paul II was named an 'Honorary Harlem Globetrotter'!"

The Globetrotters traveled to the Vatican to visit the Pontiff and personally bestow this honor upon him!

STRANGE BUT TRUE

"Camels do not carry water in their humps!"

Actually, the humps contain fat, which is stored and used as nourishment when food is scarce. Camels don't store water anywhere in their bodies contrary to popular belief!

STRANGE BUT TRUE

"The television was invented one year *BEFORE* the invention of sliced bread!"

In 1927, Philo Farnsworth, at 21 years of age, invented the television. One year later, in 1928, Otto Frederick Rohwedder of Davenport, Iowa, invented the first loaf-at-a-time bread-slicing machine.

17

STRANGE BUT TRUE

"Mr. Potato Head was the first toy to ever be advertised on TV!"

Invented by George Lerner in 1949, and manufactured by Hasbro in 1952, the original toy had plastic parts that could be stuck into a real potato. However, after complaints of rotten potatoes and new government regulations, Hasbro began including a plastic potato body with the toy set in 1964.

STRANGE BUT TRUE

"The medical name for a butt crack is 'intergluteal cleft'!"

Also known in the medical community as 'natal cleft', 'the vertical gluteal crease', and 'the gluteal cleft'. There you have it! Take your pick!

STRANGE BUT TRUE

"Before the term 'Bloopers' was coined, 'outtakes' in television, movies, and radio were called 'boners'!"

"Boners" was a word meaning a humorous mistake long before there were "Bloopers". Boners dates back to the early 1900s and is shorthand-speak for a "bone headed mistake". Nowadays, I think we all know what it refers to!

STRANGE BUT TRUE

"The term 'brain freeze' was invented by 7-11 stores to explain the pain one feels when drinking their famous 'Slurpee' too fast!"

In 1966 the 'Slurpee' was so named for the sound it made when drinking them through a straw.

'Brain Freeze' otherwise known as 'sphenopalatine ganglioneuralgia' is caused when something very cold touches the back of your throat, constricting the blood vessels and creating the intense headache known as the dreaded 'brain freeze'!

STRANGE BUT TRUE

"The man who found the 5000-year-old corpse, Otzi the Iceman in 1991, (oldest natural European mummy) was also found dead frozen in ice in 2004!"

The two German tourists, Helmut and Erika Simon found Otzi on September 19, 1991 in the Alps on the Austrian-Italian border.

Helmut, in 2004, at 67 years of age, was found frozen after falling to his death during a blizzard while hiking near the same spot he found Otzi in the ice!

STRANGE BUT TRUE

"About 40% of the people who go to a party in someone's home admit to snooping in the host's medicine cabinet!"

And about the same percentage (40%) of hosts admit that they take things out of their medicine cabinet or hide items before their guests arrive!

What are people hoping or expecting to find? Who knows! Locks on medicine cabinets may be the next big thing!

STRANGE BUT TRUE

"The Boston Marathon didn't allow female runners until 1972!"

Although not an "official" entrant, Roberta "Bobbi" Gibb became the first woman to run the Boston Marathon in 1966 and finished 126th overall.

On April 17, 1972, women were officially allowed to run the Boston Marathon and Nina Kuscsik emerged from an eight-member field to win the race in 3:10:26.

STRANGE BUT TRUE

"The man who invented pop-up ads has apologized to the world for creating one of the world's most hated forms of advertising!"

Ethan Zuckerman, the man who invented pop-up ads, says "I'm sorry."
He says it was never his intent for it to have developed into what it is today and feels the fallen state of the internet is a direct, if unintentional, consequence of choosing advertising as the default model to support online content and services.

STRANGE BUT TRUE

"Babe Ruth wore a cabbage leaf under his cap to keep him cool! He changed it every 2 innings!"

The Babe shared his 'secret technique' for staying cool with his teammates and during games they kept the cabbage leaves spread out over ice in a cooler.

STRANGE BUT TRUE

"The first film ever shown in the White House was 'The Birth of a Nation,' a pro-white supremacy silent film that the KKK also used as a recruiting tool!"

Woodrow Wilson was the President of the United States when this controversial film about slavery and the Ku Klux Klan was shown on February 18, 1915.

STRANGE BUT TRUE

"Bamboo can grow at a speed of around three feet in a day!"

Bamboo is one of the fastest growing plants in the world due to its unique rhizome-dependent system. It's much like a telescope in its growth habit as each section emerges.

STRANGE BUT TRUE

"Viagra, when dissolved in water, can make cut-flowers stay erect for up to a week longer than they usually would!"

Multiple uses for a, 'special' product!

STRANGE BUT TRUE

"If grasshoppers were the size of people, they could leap the length of a basketball court!"

The muscles they use to make their jumps have 10 times the power of the strongest human muscle cell!

STRANGE BUT TRUE

"In 2003, there were 86 days of below-freezing weather in Hell, Michigan!"

The small town near Ann Arbor embraced its newfound fame and as you can imagine, the slogan, 'Hell has Frozen Over' soon appeared on everything from t-shirts to coffee cups.

STRANGE BUT TRUE

"More Monopoly money is printed in a year, than real money printed throughout the world!"

Parker Brothers, the game's owners, reports that it prints around 30 billion in 'Monopoly Money' each year!

STRANGE BUT TRUE

"Catnip is ten-times more effective in repelling mosquitoes than DEET, the main substance used in insect repellents!"

Nepetalactone is the organic compound found in catnip that acts as an attractant to cats and also is a powerful repellant for insects, especially mosquitoes.

STRANGE BUT TRUE

"The longest span of time between the birth of twins is 87 days!"

This incredible record is held by Maria Jones-Elliot of Ireland, who gave birth to daughter Amy on June 1, 2012 and 87 days later on August 12, her twin Katie was born!

The previous record was 84 days apart when Peggy Lynn of Pennsylvania gave birth to Hanna and Eric in 1995 and 1996.

STRANGE BUT TRUE

"The world's termites outweigh the world's people!"

If you combine the total mass of all the termites in the world, they would weigh more than the total combined mass of the world's 7 billion humans!

STRANGE BUT TRUE

"In 2014, Netflix spent $0 on marketing its DVD rental business, but over 6 million people still used it!"

Started in 1997, Netflix, by 2016 had over 80 million subscribers, roughly the same as the population of Germany!

STRANGE BUT TRUE

"Hawaii's state flag is the only US state flag to feature the Union Jack upon it!"

In 1793, Captain George Vancouver from Great Britain presented the Union Jack to King Kamehameha I, who was uniting the islands into a single independent kingdom. The Union Jack flew unofficially as the flag of Hawaii until 1816. The flag of Great Britain is currently emblazoned in the upper left corner of Hawaii's flag to honor Hawaii's friendship with Britain.

STRANGE BUT TRUE

"Istanbul, Turkey is the only city in the world located on two continents!"

Istanbul, Turkey is located on both the continent of Europe, known as Thrace, and the continent of Asia, known as Asia Minor. Istanbul's European part is separated from its Asian part by the Bosphorus Strait, a waterway that connects the Black Sea with the Sea of Marmara, forming a natural boundary between the two continents.

38

STRANGE BUT TRUE

"The king of hearts is the only king without a moustache on a deck of standard playing cards!"

He originally had one but lost it in the reproduction process of the original design over the years. Same thing happened to the axe he is holding, now appearing as a sword pointed at his head.

STRANGE BUT TRUE

"The first microwave oven was almost as tall as a refrigerator!"

In 1947, Raytheon Corporation built the "Radarange", the first commercially available microwave oven. It was almost 6 feet tall and weighed 750 pounds!

STRANGE BUT TRUE

"It takes glass one million years to decompose, which means it never wears out and can be recycled an infinite number of times!"

Glass alone makes up 5% of all the garbage in the U.S. Recycling glass containers just makes good sense environmentally and economically.

STRANGE BUT TRUE

"7-Up, invented in 1920, contained lithium, the drug now commonly prescribed to sufferers of bipolar disorder!"

The soft drink, created in 1929 by Charles Grigg of St. Louis, it was originally named "Bib-Label Lithiated Lemon-Lime Soda". During that era, Lithium Citrate was considered to be a healthy additive and was believed to have curative powers. 7-Up, along with several others during this time, were part of a trend of 'medicated soft drinks'.

STRANGE BUT TRUE

"Some of the first soles on Nike shoes were made by pouring rubber into a waffle iron!"

In 1964, track star Bill Knight and his coach, Bill Bowerman, founded Blue Ribbon Sports (now known as Nike). In 1970, Bill Bowerman's desire to improve upon the shoe design, led him to use the family's waffle iron, pouring rubber into it to create the prototype for the now famous 'Nike Waffle Outsole'.

STRANGE BUT TRUE

"There are no clocks in Las Vegas gambling casinos!"

It's pretty widely accepted that the reason for this is that by not having clocks in view, players will be in a hyper-focus state of mind, lose track of time, and play longer.

STRANGE BUT TRUE

"Spoons are a millennium older than forks!"

Unlike forks, that for the most part had to be fashioned, natural spoons could be utilized by using such ready-made things as animal bones, seashells and stones. Spoons with handles were used in ancient Egypt as early as 1000 BC.

STRANGE BUT TRUE

"The term 'deadline' comes from the American Civil War. Prisoners would have lines drawn around them in the dirt, and if they crossed this line they'd be executed by their guards. Prisoners and guards soon began calling this line the, 'deadline'!"

In modern times people still often avoid and fear 'deadlines'!

STRANGE BUT TRUE

"2003 was the year 'bootylicious' and 'bitch-slap' were added to the dictionary!"

The term 'bootylicious' was first used by rapper Snoop Dogg in his song in 1992. The popularity of the song caused the term to become widespread and added to the dictionary.

The term, 'bitch-slap' became popular around 1990 and quickly became widely used as a reference to slapping someone with an expression of dominance, contempt, or disrespect.

STRANGE BUT TRUE

"Colombian drug-lord, Pablo Escobar kept four hippos on his estate before his death in 1993. Proving too difficult to remove by authorities, the hippos were left there, have since bred and escaped, becoming an invasive species in Colombia!"

The Columbian government is concerned about the danger posed to people and damage to the ecosystem since the hippos have no predators in Columbia as they do in Africa and their population is increasing uncontrollably.

STRANGE BUT TRUE

"The first Rolls Royce, sold for about $785 in 1906. Now it would be about $295,000!"

In 1904, Charles Rolls and Henry Royce partnered and founded Rolls-Royce Limited. Their reputation for hand-building some of the finest automobiles in the world has made them legends – and their creations extremely valuable and sought after!

STRANGE BUT TRUE

"In Tokyo, a bicycle is faster than a car for most trips of less than 50 minutes!"

Traffic congestion in Tokyo is legendary, and unless you want to sit in your car going nowhere fast- consider riding a bicycle. You'll arrive ahead of everyone else!

STRANGE BUT TRUE

"The names of Popeye's four nephews are Pip-eye, Peep-eye, Pup-eye, and Poop-eye!"

The hugely popular cartoon character, 'Popeye the Sailor', was probably the reason any kid ever ate his spinach, as that is what gave Popeye his strength. Popeye's four nephews, apparently quadruplets, made their first appearance in the 1942 short, 'Pip-eye, Pup-eye, Poop-eye an' Peep-eye'.

STRANGE BUT TRUE

"Artist Salvador Dali would often get out of paying for drinks and meals by drawing on the cheques, making them priceless works of art, and therefore un-cashable!"

With his wild art and a personality to match, Salvador Dali, the Spanish surrealist, enjoyed indulging in unusual and grandiose behavior and attention-grabbing public antics!

STRANGE BUT TRUE

"Tattoo coloring (Acrylonitrile butadiene styrene) is also what LEGOs are made out of!"

Some of the most popular pigments found in tattoo inks are made from ABS, the heat-resistant plastic used to make luggage, appliance parts, LEGOs, and when ground down, tattoo inks. These types of inks are very popular because of the vivid colors they produce.

STRANGE BUT TRUE

"Mosquitoes kill 72,500 times more people around the world each year than sharks!"

On average, 725,000 people around the world die each year of diseases like Malaria, West Nile virus and the Zika virus from mosquito bites compared to deaths from shark attacks which number around 10!

STRANGE BUT TRUE

"In the 1700s, barbers not only gave haircuts and shaves but also pulled teeth, performed surgery and did bloodletting!"

These 'barber surgeons' as they were called, performed these procedures primarily on the war wounded. As time went on however, they were limited to just pulling teeth and bloodletting.

STRANGE BUT TRUE

"While children of identical twins are legally first cousins, they are actually half siblings!"

Which is why identical twins are also called monozygotic. Since they both have the same DNA, this is almost like the two sets of children have the same moms but different dads. In fact, this is why at the DNA level they are really more like half siblings than first cousins.

STRANGE BUT TRUE

"The first animals in space were fruit flies, launched in a V-2 rocket by the U.S. in 1947. The fruit flies were recovered alive!"

The fruit flies were launched in a Nazi designed V-2 rocket and reached an altitude of 67 miles above the Earth – 1 mile into what is considered where 'space' begins and were recovered alive by parachute in New Mexico. A main reason fruit flies were chosen is that approximately 75% of the disease-causing genes in humans have analogues in the fruit fly's genetic code.

STRANGE BUT TRUE

"The world's largest pyramid is not in Egypt. It's in Cholula, Puebla near Mexico City!"

The 'Great Pyramid of Cholula' is the largest pyramid in the world standing at 217 feet tall and a total volume of 4.45 million cubic meters.

By contrast, the Great Pyramid of Giza in Egypt, is higher at 455 feet tall, but only has a total volume of 2.5 million cubic meters.

STRANGE BUT TRUE

"In 2008, Microsoft had offered to buy Yahoo for US$44.6 billion. Yahoo rejected the offer. In 2016, it was sold for just US$4.8 billion!"

Microsoft had offered then CEO, Jerry Yang $31 per share but Yang turned it down. Later that year, Yahoo shares dipped below $10 per share.
In 2016, Yahoo was bought by Verizon for $4.8 billion. A lot of Microsoft investors breathe easier knowing that their initial offer to Yahoo didn't happen!

STRANGE BUT TRUE

"Fingernails grow more than twice as fast as toenails!"

A fingernail replaces itself in about 6 months, while a toenail takes about a year. Scientists are unsure of the reason for this difference, but one theory is that our toenails are further away from our heart than our fingernails and most likely receive less circulation.

STRANGE BUT TRUE

"Most dust particles in people's homes are from dead skin!"

It's estimated that from 70 to 80 % of all the dust in people's homes are actually made up of dead skin cells. Other sources that make up the remainder can come from pet dander, soil particles tracked in from outside, and carpet fibers, bedding, and furniture.

STRANGE BUT TRUE

"Bullet proof vests, fire escapes, windshield wipers and the dishwasher were all invented by women!"

Kevlar Bullet Proof Vests – Stephanie Kwolek in 1965.

Fire Escapes with Staircase - Anna Connelly in 1887.

Windshield Wipers – Mary Anderson in 1903.

Dishwasher – Josephine Cochrane in 1886.

STRANGE BUT TRUE

"Water is the thing most often choked on by Americans!"

Believe it or not, water is the culprit, due to its being a thin liquid it's often gulped and subsequently choked on.

STRANGE BUT TRUE

"The creator of the board game 'Monopoly', intended the game to demonstrate that monopolies are bad for society!"

In 1903, Elizabeth Magie created the game of Monopoly. She hoped and intended for it to be an educational tool to illustrate the negative effects of concentrating land in private monopolies.

STRANGE BUT TRUE

"The first product to have a bar code was Wrigley's gum!"

At 8:01am on June 26, 1974, a 10-pack of Wrigley Juicy Fruit gum became the first item ever scanned for its barcode at a Marsh supermarket in Troy, Ohio.

The scanner now resides at the Smithsonian National Museum of American History.

STRANGE BUT TRUE

"The sentence 'The quick brown fox jumps over a lazy dog' uses every letter of the alphabet!"

A pangram, or holoalphabetic sentence, is a sentence that contains every letter of the alphabet at least once. Probably the most famous pangram is the one above which was used to test typewriters since the 1800s.

STRANGE BUT TRUE

"Before toothpaste was invented, some people cleaned their teeth with Charcoal!"

In the early 1800s, ground charcoal became a popular 'home-made toothpaste' for people to brush their teeth with. Over the years many different ingredients have been used in toothpastes and 'activated charcoal' is still one of them!

STRANGE BUT TRUE

"A man once sued Warner Brothers, and won, after he was injured while fainting during a screening of 'The Exorcist'!"

A filmgoer, who was watching the movie in 1974, fainted and broke his jaw on the seat in front of him. He sued Warner Brothers, claiming that the use of subliminal imagery in the film had caused him to pass out.
The film affected audiences so strongly that paramedics were called frequently to theaters to treat people who fainted and went into hysterics.

STRANGE BUT TRUE

"The chance that a dollar bill contains remnants of cocaine is 80%!"

A single bill used to snort cocaine or otherwise mingled with the drug can contaminate an entire cash drawer. When counting and sorting machines (which fans the bills and thus the cocaine) are factored in, it's no wonder that so much of the currency now in circulation wouldn't pass any purity tests.

STRANGE BUT TRUE

"Spiked and studded dog collars derive from the ancient Greeks, who put these collars on their sheep-dogs to protect their necks from wolves while they watched over the flock at night!"

In modern times, spiked collars, whether worn by dogs or their owners, are more of a trendy fashion statement, symbolizing protection and ferocity.

STRANGE BUT TRUE

In 2012, Afghan Taliban Commander
Mohammed Ashan turned himself in
to local authorities, trying to claim the
$100 reward he had seen on a
poster for his arrest!"

Afghan and U.S. forces were
dumbfounded when Ashan
surrendered. Up until now, the tactic
of using 'wanted' posters for
insurgents hadn't yielded many
positive results.

STRANGE BUT TRUE

"A mosquito's saliva acts as an anesthetic so you usually don't notice when one bites you!"

It also serves as an anticoagulant to keep her proboscis (her mouth) from becoming clogged and keep your blood flowing so she can get her fill!

STRANGE BUT TRUE

"The Pentagon has no marble because it was built during World War II, and Italy, the source of marble, was an enemy country of the U.S. in WWII!"

Constructed primarily of reinforced concrete, it was built using the 'Stripped Classicism' style of architecture which lacks most or all ornamentation and was popular for government buildings during this timeframe.

STRANGE BUT TRUE

"The man who took the famous photo of the Wright Brothers' first flight had never used a camera before that day!"

On December 17, 1903, John Thomas Daniels, Jr. used a Gundlach Korona view camera with a five-by-seven-inch glass-plate negative to take the famous photo. Daniels said later that he was so excited to see the Wright Flyer rising that he almost forgot to squeeze the bulb to trigger the shutter!

STRANGE BUT TRUE

"The average life span of a major league baseball is 5-7 pitches!"

Major League Baseball reports that approximately 157,950 baseballs are used every season at a cost of around 5.5 million dollars!

STRANGE BUT TRUE

"The song, 'I Gotta Feeling' by the Black Eyed Peas sold more copies than any Elvis Presley single when it was released!"

At almost 9 million downloads, it holds the record as the most downloaded song on iTunes of all time. This also makes it the highest selling digital as well as non-charity single in the US ever.

STRANGE BUT TRUE

"At least 100 rocks from Mars have landed on Earth!"

Rocks from Mars, 'Martian Meteorites', are formed and ejected from Mars by the impact of an asteroid or comet. Of over 61,000 meteorites that have been found on Earth, 132 were identified as having come from Mars.

STRANGE BUT TRUE

"From groundbreaking to opening day, Disneyland was built in just 365 days!"

Opened on July 17, 1955, in Anaheim, California, it was designed and built to completion under the direct supervision of Walt Disney himself.

STRANGE BUT TRUE

"In the U.S., staged wrestling is called 'professional wrestling' while real wrestling is called 'amateur wrestling'!"

'Professional Wrestling' became a phenomenon in the 1980s with the expansion of the World Wrestling Federation catering to their fans love of theatrics and showmanship.

'Amateur Wrestling' gained popularity after the US Civil war. USA Wrestling is the organization that governs wresting in the United States and is the official representative to the US Olympic Committee.

STRANGE BUT TRUE

"In its first 4 months of sales in 1958, over 25 million Hula Hoops were sold!"

Richard Knerr and Arthur Melin of the Wham-O Company hold the trademark on the name, 'Hula Hoop' and initially sold them for $1.98 each!

STRANGE BUT TRUE

"Windmills always turn counter-clockwise. Except for the windmills in Ireland!"

If a windmill is facing the opposite of the wind direction, it will turn counter-clockwise. If the blades are faced into the wind, they'll turn clockwise.

STRANGE BUT TRUE

"The placement of a donkey's eyes in its head enables it to see all four feet at the same time!"

This peripheral vison gives them an almost 360-degree view of their surroundings.

Donkeys are very strong, highly intelligent, keenly aware of their surroundings, and rarely spook like a horse will, if caught by surprise.

STRANGE BUT TRUE

"The U.S.-Canada border is the longest border in the world without a military defense!"

These 5,525 miles create the world's longest shared border. The historical and cultural heritage shared by these countries has resulted in one of the most stable and mutually beneficial relationships in the world.

STRANGE BUT TRUE

"Captain Kirk never actually said the phrase, 'Beam me up Scotty' in any Star Trek episode!"

He did however come very close with a few variations such as, "beam me up" and "Scotty, beam me up."

STRANGE BUT TRUE

"'Take Your Houseplants for a Walk Day' is celebrated on July 27th, whereas people walk their houseplants around so they (houseplants) can get to know their environment a little more, which supposedly provides the plants with a sense of familiarization with their surrounding areas!"

This 'special' day was invented by Thomas and Ruth Roy. OK.

STRANGE BUT TRUE

"Tomatoes were thought to be poisonous until the 1800s!"

The tomato is native to western South America. Wild versions were small, like cherry tomatoes. A member of the deadly nightshade family, tomatoes were erroneously thought to be poisonous by Europeans who were suspicious of their bright, shiny fruit.

STRANGE BUT TRUE

"The word 'Gorilla' comes from a Greek word that means 'a tribe of hairy women'!"

Hanno the Navigator, (c. 500 BC) a Carthaginian explorer, who while on an expedition on the west African coast to the area that later became known as Sierra Leone, encountered and named these creatures. The name Hanno used was derived from Ancient Greek, meaning 'tribe of hairy women'.

STRANGE BUT TRUE

"Commonly thought to be an ancient Greek tradition, the Olympic torch relay was actually a Nazi idea!"

The Olympic torch relay began in 1936 at the Berlin Games. Carl Diem, the secretary general of the Organizing Committee of the games of the XI Olympiad in Berlin, proposed using a torch relay to bring the flame from Olympia, Greece, to the games in Berlin, Germany.

STRANGE BUT TRUE

"Australia is the only continent in the world without an active volcano!"

There are about 1500 potentially active volcanoes worldwide not counting the ones on the ocean floor. About 500 volcanoes have erupted throughout historical time. Many of these are located along the Pacific Rim in what is known as the 'Ring of Fire.'

STRANGE BUT TRUE

"According to the FDA, the stickers on fruit are edible!"

It's recommended by the FDA to wash all fruit before eating, but if you also eat the stickers on fruit, don't worry, they won't hurt you. The stickers and their adhesive are FDA-approved and safe to ingest if you're so inclined!

STRANGE BUT TRUE

"The cigarette lighter was invented before the match was invented!"

In 1823, a German chemist named Johann Wolfgang Dobereiner invented the first lighter.

The match was invented in 1826, three years later, by English chemist John Walker.

STRANGE BUT TRUE

"In addition to cigarettes, nicotine was used in insecticides!"

Nicotine is naturally found in the nightshade family of plants and around 2-14% in tobacco plant leaves.
After World War II, over 2,500 tons of nicotine insecticide was used worldwide. Due to cheaper and safer alternatives, it has not been available as a pesticide since 2014 in the United States.

STRANGE BUT TRUE

"A California man obtained a license plate that said 'NO PLATE' and received more than 2500 parking tickets!"

All the Los Angeles man wanted was his own 'personalized' plates he said, but after seven years and over 2500 citations he still wonders if it was the right choice. Countless letters to the courts explaining the mix-up eventually cleared up the matter and he became a bit of a local celebrity!

STRANGE BUT TRUE

"A lightning bolt strikes so fast it could circle the globe eight times in one second!"

Lightning travels at a speed of about 320,000,000 feet per second or about 220,000,000 miles per hour (about 1/3 the speed of light). In comparison, the sound of thunder travels at about 1100 feet per second or about 750 miles per hour.

STRANGE BUT TRUE

"Applesauce was the first food eaten in space by an American astronaut!"

John Glenn, the first American astronaut to eat in space, had applesauce during the Friendship 7 flight in 1962. While Glenn said he had no problem swallowing or digesting the food, he did say it wasn't very delicious!

STRANGE BUT TRUE

"Banging your head against a wall burns 150 calories an hour!"

If that isn't exactly your idea of a good time, perhaps try going for a nice walk, where you'll burn about 170 calories an hour.
Your choice!

STRANGE BUT TRUE

"The tongue of a Blue Whale weighs more than most elephants!"

Blue Whales, the largest animals ever known to live on Earth, have tongues that can weigh up to 8000 pounds! That's the equivalent of an entire adult Elephant!

STRANGE BUT TRUE

"Walt Disney World Resort
encompasses 30,500 acres, making
it approximately the same size as
San Francisco!"

The property consists of 40 square
miles! That's equal to the size of
San Francisco or two Manhattan's!
Located just southwest of Orlando,
Florida, Walt Disney and his brother
Roy, started purchasing various
tracts of land in 1965 totaling
$5,018,770.00!

98

STRANGE BUT TRUE

"65% of test subjects had the urge to yawn after merely reading about yawning!"

Here are a few things that make me yawn; political ads on TV, hearing about your operation, seeing someone yawn, and yes, Daylight Savings Time!

STRANGE BUT TRUE

"Abraham Lincoln's body has been buried, exhumed, inspected, or reburied at least 17 times since his death!"

Following his assassination on April 15, 1865, and burial on May 4, 1865, Abraham Lincoln's remains were first moved on December 21, 1865 from Oak Ridge Cemetery and subsequently moved 16 more times, before finally finding his final resting place on September 26, 1901 in the Catacomb, Lincoln Tomb in Springfield, Illinois.

STRANGE BUT TRUE

"The Leaning Tower of Pisa started tilting before the building was ever completed!"

The Leaning Tower of Pisa, in Italy, is known worldwide for its unintended tilt. The tower's tilt began during construction in the 12th century and increased in the decades that followed before it was eventually completed in the 14th century. The famous tilt was caused by a foundation that was built on ground too soft on one side to support the Towers weight, which is estimated at 14,500 metric tons!

STRANGE BUT TRUE

"King Charles I, the monarch of England, Scotland, and Ireland in the 1600s, favorite joke, was to place his 18-inch-tall court dwarf between two halves of bread and pretend to eat him!"

Known by the nickname of Lord Minimus, he was nine years old when his father presented him to King Charles I. According to the story he wasn't so much 'presented' to the King as he was 'served' to the King in a pie!
The King and Queen took a liking to him and he became a source of amusement at the King's Court!

ABOUT THE AUTHOR

Michael Schlueter is an author and photographer living with his wife Jill and their two pup dogs on a small farm in Missouri. He enjoys spending time in the great outdoors, seeing new places, and sharing laughs with family and friends.

Other books by Michael include, *"101 Quirky & Crazy Phrases & Sayings"* and the coffee-table fine art photography book, *"America's Bloodiest 47 Acres - Inside the Missouri State Penitentiary"*.

Visit Michael and see more of his work at:

www.schlueterphoto.com
www.amazon.com/author/michaelschlueter